ARMY
RISE UP

Strategies to Equip God's Soldiers

JUDITH GAFFNEY

WESTBOW
PRESS®
A DIVISION OF THOMAS NELSON
& ZONDERVAN

WestBow Press books may be ordered through booksellers or by contacting:

WestBow Press
A Division of Thomas Nelson & Zondervan
1663 Liberty Drive
Bloomington, IN 47403
www.westbowpress.com
844-714-3454

Scripture taken from the King James Version of the Bible.

ISBN: 978-1-6642-4609-6 (sc)
ISBN: 978-1-6642-4608-9 (hc)
ISBN: 978-1-6642-4610-2 (e)

Library of Congress Control Number: 2021920101

Print information available on the last page.

WestBow Press rev. date: 06/16/2022

For the weapons of our warfare are not carnal, but mighty through God to the pulling down of strongholds.
—2 Corinthians 10:4

In 2020, during the Covid-19 pandemic, God inspired me to write this book to encourage other warriors in Christ. He showed me key tools that will prepare us for this new era and the times to come. These tools are necessary to be effective and impactful. After you read this book, I believe that you will be encouraged to strategically advance God's kingdom and to walk in another level of love, authority, and dominion.

INTRODUCTION

In late December 2019, while driving on the Northern State Parkway to teach a Bible study for young adults, I heard the Spirit of the Lord say that 2020 would be a year of horses and chariots. This startled me because I knew that horses and chariots meant warfare.

When I arrived at the Bible study, I was happy to see so many young adults. I knew God was going to move mightily and that they came with an expectancy to hear from Him. After I finished teaching the lesson, a young woman I didn't know shared that she had been tormented by demons and how God delivered her. She said during her deliverance process, she had a vision of God sending horses and chariots to save her. This was confirmation. God had just spoken to me about 2020 being a year of horses and chariots. That night was an awesome demonstration of God's power. Many asked for prayer, and God poured out His love on them.

The next day during our Sunday service, I shared that God said the year 2020 would be a year of horses and chariots. Everyone seemed attentive, and I knew God was preparing us for something. A few days later, the Holy Spirit spoke to my heart and said to tell the church that not only were we to fast for the month of January 2020, but that every day during the entire year, we should have prayer on the conference line. God prepared us for the warfare that was ahead and kept us through the entire year, after much prayer and fasting, as "we kept our heads to the ground".

During the quarantine in March 2020, God spoke to my heart about the need for His army, the church, to arise. He told me to write a book with key tools that will help train and build the army for the days and years ahead. I believe that this book will equip you to arise and encourage you to walk in your purpose.

DEDICATION

I dedicate this book to my Lord and Savior, Jesus Christ, Who is the real author.

My husband, Cyernard D. Gaffney, has always inspired me to pursue my dreams. I thank God for Cyernard because he is such a joyful person and a pleasure to be with. He has made my journey so much easier because of his wisdom and sense of humor.

I also dedicate this book to my mother, the late Jean Elizabeth Broadway, who laid the foundation of Jesus in our home, and to my father, the late Charles Freeman Broadway, who encouraged me to study hard and pursue business administration.

My children, Moriah, Ramah, and Jordan, are the answer to my prayers. I asked God to give us twins and a son. I know you are warriors and influencers for the kingdom of God.

To my sister, Karen Broadway-Wilson: I love you. You are so supportive and encourage me in everything I do. You are a wonderful, beautiful sister and a great friend.

To my brothers, Chuck and Brian Broadway: You are inspirations. You have influenced and facilitated change for so many lives in your community with the love and wisdom of God. I see the prayers of our mother manifested through your lives.

To my stepsister, Jeanine Broadway: You are a warrior in Jesus.

To my brother-in-law, Pastor Michael Wilson, Bridges Worldwide Ministries, and Dr. Renee Woods from Fresh Wind Ministries, thank you all for your prayers and support.

CHAPTER 1

YOU ARE LOVED AND COMMISSIONED

Know and believe what God thinks about you. He is the most important person in the universe. He loves you with an eternal love. He is with you always.

> Teaching them to observe all things whatsoever I have commanded you: and, lo, I am with you always, even unto the end of the world. Amen. (Matthew 28:20)

> Let your conversation be without covetousness; and be content with such things as ye have: for he hath said, I will never leave thee, nor forsake thee. (Hebrews 13:5)

> But ye are a chosen generation, a royal priesthood, an holy nation, a peculiar people;

that ye should shew forth the praises of him who hath called you out of darkness into his marvelous light. In time past, we were not a people but are now the people of God, which had not obtained mercy, but now have obtained mercy. (1 Peter 2:9–10)

You have been commissioned by God because He loves you.

How can warriors be victorious when they don't understand the heart of the commander-in-chief? We must know in our hearts that God's love is perfect toward us and His plans for our life originated in love. God is love, and everything about Him is saturated in love.

There may have been a time in your life when you equated our heavenly Father with your natural father. If you didn't have a good relationship with your biological father, it could be easy to subconsciously feel that God can't be a good father because your earthly father is the point of reference. Perhaps your earthly father was abusive or wasn't supportive. Maybe he abandoned you. The painful experiences you may have had can affect your perspective of God. If you had a good relationship with your earthly father, then you must realize that if he was there to help you and give you good things, how much more your heavenly Father will give you the best from His eternal kingdom.

Therefore, it is crucial on the battlefield to know you have a heavenly Father Whose love is perfect for you. What does perfect mean? Free from fault or error; complete and absolute. He gave His only begotten Son, Jesus, to die for our sins. Jesus, Who knew no sin, became sin for us so we would be made the righteousness of God in the earth. Imagine this kind of love for you. Jesus became what His Father hated so we would be who His Father loved. Jesus was the perfect sacrifice for our sins.

Take a moment, and think about this amazing love expressed for you through Jesus. God gave us all He had so we could have a victorious, abundant, and eternal life. His love will never fade. His love is eternal. The love of God is unselfish, incomprehensible, and not understood by the carnal mind. Jesus was sent from the Father to bring us back to the relationship our heavenly Father wanted from the beginning. You are loved by the greatest person on earth and in heaven. He has promised to never leave you or forsake you. What a wonderful relationship we have with God through Jesus Christ. It is crucial to know that God is for you and with you always. As the days get darker, we have to know in our hearts that God's love towards us will never change or cease.

There was a season in my life when I felt like God didn't hear my prayers. I felt alone, abandoned, and disappointed. Despite how I felt, I kept talking to God. I expressed my disappointment, even though I was upset with Him. I don't know how God did it, but He rescued me from myself. I was drowning in sadness. God will never give up on you. He loves you. No matter how difficult the situation is or how distraught you may feel, keep talking to Jesus. He will rescue you. God's love will lift you, remove the burdens, and restore joy and peace in your heart.

Army Workout Exercises

1. Did you grow up having a supportive father? If so, describe him.
2. List and discuss three characteristics of a good father.
3. Find at least three scriptures that show the attributes of God as a great Father.
4. Make a decision to talk to Jesus every day, and take time to listen to Him. For five days, journal your conversation with Jesus.

Know Who You Are

When we fully comprehend in our spirit, not in our human intellect, who we are, we become an unstoppable, unshakeable weapon against powers of darkness.

In order to handle the challenges of this new era, we have to understand our identity in Christ. We must know who we are. God's love letter and road map is the Bible. It is explicit about our identity. We must do more than just read the Word; we must study it and meditate on it. The Word of God must saturate our minds and affect our motives. The Word of God is supernatural.

"It is the spirit that quickeneth; the flesh profiteth nothing: the words that I speak unto you, they are spirit, and they are life" (John 6:63).

Our identity in Christ is always under attack. The adversary doesn't want us to fully comprehend who God has made us to be in the earth. John 10:10 says that the devil has come to steal, kill, and destroy, but Jesus came so that we might have life and have it more abundantly. Pronounce this over your life right now: "I have abundant life in Jesus. I have more than enough in Jesus. My life is full and complete in Jesus." Say those words, and more importantly, believe them and live like you believe them.

The enemy will try to influence your thoughts with things that are false. It is important to have your mind renewed daily by studying the word of God. God's word defines who we are and will destroy the darts of deceptive and toxic thinking. When we stand by faith in God's Word, we are arsenal against his kingdom and effective change agents in the earth. Greater is He Who is in you than he who is in the world. Know what God says about you in the core of your being, and live like you know Who your Father is.

The spirit of this world wants us to retreat and surrender our rights. We must resist the devil by being fully persuaded of our identity in Jesus and having our hearts committed to His Word. When we know who we are according to God's Word, it prepares us to stand against the arrows of hell that aim to pierce our minds. These arrows sent from hell are lies. They want us to think we are not worthy of God's grace, love, and kindness.

The lies from hell remind us of things we have done; they want to keep us in cycles of guilt and shame. Rise up, and remind yourself and the voices from the enemy that you are the righteousness of Christ in the earth. Say it: "Jesus has redeemed me with His own blood and made me righteous. I am the righteousness of Christ in the Earth. I am forgiven from my past, and I am free." God is truth. It is impossible for Him to lie. The principalities and powers in this world have no weight in God's kingdom. What God has said is final and eternal. We are forever blessed in Jesus, and nothing can stop His Word over our lives.

What God Says About You

You are a world influencer: "Ye are the light of the world. A city that is set on a hill cannot be hid" (Matthew 5:14).

Greatness is in you: "Ye are of God, little children, and have overcome them: because greater is he that is in you than he that is in the world" (1 John 4:4).

You are an overcomer: "These things I have spoken unto you, that in me ye might have peace. In the world ye shall have tribulation: but be of good cheer; I have overcome the world" (John 16:33).

You are redeemed and have the blessings of Abraham: "Christ has redeemed us from the curse of the law, being made a curse for us, for it is written, cursed is every one that hangeth on a tree;

"That the blessing of Abraham might come on the Gentiles through Jesus Christ; that we might receive the promise of the Spirit through faith" (Galatians 3:13-14).

You are a royal priesthood: "But ye *are* a chosen generation, a royal priesthood, an holy nation, a peculiar people; that ye should shew forth the praises of him who hath called you out of darkness into his marvellous light" (1 Peter 2:9).

You are a minister of reconciliation: "And all things *are* of God, who hath reconciled us to himself by Jesus Christ, and hath given to us the ministry of reconciliation" (1 Corinthians 5:18).

You are a partaker of a divine nature: "Whereby are given unto us exceeding great and precious promises: that by these ye might be partakers of the divine nature, having escaped the corruption that is in the world through lust" (2 Peter 1:4).

You are complete in Jesus: "And ye are complete in him, which is the head of all principality and power" (Colossians 2:10).

Jesus made you complete. *Complete* is defined as "to fill to the top; lacking nothing; having all necessary parts; thorough; making something perfect or whole."

You are more than a conqueror: "Nay, in all these things we are more than conquerors through him that loved us" (Romans 8:37).

You are not condemned: "There is therefore now no condemnation to them which are in Christ Jesus, who walk not after the flesh, but after the Spirit" (Romans 8:1).

You have the spirit of love, the power, and a sound mind: "For God hath not given us the spirit of fear; but of power, and of love, and of a sound mind" (2 Timothy 1:7).

You are a temple of the Holy Spirit: "What? know ye not that your body is the temple of the Holy Ghost, which is in you, which ye have of God, and ye are not your own? For ye are bought with a price: therefore, glorify God in your body, and in your spirit, which are God's" (1 Corinthians 6:19–20).

You are joint heirs with Jesus Christ: "And if children, then heirs; heirs of God, and joint-heirs with Christ; if so be that we suffer with him, that we may be also glorified together" (Romans 8:17).

You are victorious: "But thanks be to God, which giveth us the victory through our Lord Jesus Christ" (1 Corinthians 15:57).

You are the righteousness of Christ: "For he hath made him to be sin for us, who knew no sin; that we might be made the righteousness of God in him" (2 Corinthians 5:21).

You are never forsaken: "Let your conversation be without covetousness; and be content with such things as ye have: for he hath said, I will never leave thee, nor forsake thee" (Hebrews 13:5).

You have the most powerful person who loves you in your life: God "hath spoken once; twice have I heard this; that power belongeth unto God" (Psalm 62:11).

"He that loveth not knoweth not God; for God is love" (1 John 4:8).

God cares for you: "Casting all your care upon him; for he careth for you" (1 Peter 5:7).

You are free: "If the Son therefore shall make you free, ye shall be free indeed" (John 8:36).

Prayer for awareness

Holy Spirit, you are the Spirit of truth. Open the eyes of my heart so that I understand, appreciate, and celebrate who God has made me to be.

Testimony and Reflection

In 2018, God put it on my heart to start a business selling African-inspired garments. I thought this was very odd because even though I always loved fashion, I was never particularly interested in African styles. I always shied away from things that would appear as being African-centric. It wasn't that I didn't like the clothing, because I travelled to Africa and purchased many beautiful garments there. I felt as if the African American culture wasn't valued, and things related to my history weren't seen as important in society. So, I took on the same mindset and worked hard to fit in.

God used my business, Culture Trees Designs, to deliver my heart from not appreciating and celebrating who He designed me to be (He's still doing this). As I researched the fabric types and designs for my business, I learned about Africa's rich culture and history. The bodacious colors, motifs, and geometric prints tell a story of struggle, faith, and victory. I was very surprised when I participated in the New York Fashion Week and other fashion shows, that producers and models from many different ethnicities loved the collections. I remember when one of the models, who wasn't African American, asked me to meet her in Manhattan to purchase one of my colorful Ankara-print coats.

I didn't choose to be a black woman; God did. He made me who I am, and everything He does is great. He does not make mistakes. His ways are perfect toward us. If we allow the world to set the bar for what is valuable, we will be deceived and miss out on experiences God wants us to have. I believe we are one in Christ, and He doesn't look at the outer appearance but looks at the heart. Jesus wants us to do the same. God placed me and you on this earth in a skin color for a purpose. The purpose is not to live a life of entitlement or oppression, but to show His love and break barriers. I believe God is intentional; He doesn't do things haphazardly. He places your spirit in a human body to fulfill a divine assignment on earth. There are benefits that I must obtain in the spirit and in the natural while navigating in this human body on planet earth. God does all things well, and I will not deny who He has created me to be, and you shouldn't either. Let's learn how to celebrate our differences and appreciate them. It's time for believers to appreciate how God has made His body so diverse and celebrate the awesomeness of His creative power.

Army Workout Exercises

1. How would you describe yourself? Write three things you like about yourself and three areas in your life that you want to improve.

2. List and discuss three scriptures that describe your identity in Christ.

3. Are you persuaded that what God says about you is true? Why or why not?

CHAPTER 2

KNOW WHY YOU ARE HERE

Chaotic times, social and economic upheaval, political unrest, and racial tensions are increasing and will continue to disrupt societal norms. You are alive because there is something you must do. God created you to fulfill a purpose on earth. Your life matters, and you are not just here to fill up space or take up time. Your skin color, the texture of your hair, your nose and facial features were beautifully planned and created in love by our heavenly Father. He doesn't make mistakes, and He knew you before you were born: "Before I formed thee in the belly, I knew thee, and before thou camest forth out of the womb I sanctified thee, and ordained thee a prophet unto nations" (Jeremiah 1:5).

We were created in God's likeness and image to reflect His love and glory in the earth. When people look at believers, they should see something different. They should see the character of Jesus. We are called to be salt and light in the earth. With Jesus we are "game changers". This may sound familiar, but it is our reality. God designed us to be the greatest influencers in the earth. What are influencers? They are people with credibility who have an established audience and can persuade others by virtue of their trustworthiness and authenticity.

When Jesus saved us, we were filled with the Holy Spirit. We have God's spirit living in us to show us the truth. You are the authentic one. You are the one God designed to manifest His love and light in the world. God is love, and there are no substitutes. He is the real deal. We cannot allow this world to cause us to think that we are lost when we have the answer. It is important for us to know what we are assigned to do in the earth and walk out that plan, with God's assistance. Everything in this world is temporal. God is eternal; He wants us to know our eternal purpose. It's time for you to live your best life, and that begins with seeking God for His wisdom and instructions. He knows why He created you and what you were designed to do.

> While we look not at the things which are seen, but at the things which are not seen: for the things which are seen are temporal; but the things which are not seen are eternal. (2 Corinthians 4:18)

God breathed into Adam the breath of life, and he became a living soul. God's breath caused Adam to become alive and aware of his purpose. Adam's purpose was to commune with God, steward the Garden of Eden, multiply and replenish the earth. God's breath in us gives life and activates His creative power. He created us to do something in the earth that will glorify Him and demonstrate His love to others. If you are not sure why you are here, right now, ask the Holy Spirit to reveal your purpose. We were designed to manifest extraordinary, supernatural greatness. What does that statement imply? You are not just on planet earth to exist, but you are here to accomplish an assignment that was written with clear instructions and strategies. Despite the hurt, pain, rejection, deceit, confusion, and other things that deter you, the purpose of God cannot be nullified. Take a moment, and say this to yourself:

"I am still here.

"I have a purpose.

"I have a great destiny.

"I am victorious.

"I am a miracle."

Pause one moment and think about your life. You know your "real" testimony. God's grace and mercy has kept you alive. Give God praise!

Prayer for Awareness

Holy Spirit, the Spirit of truth, remove all blinders from my eyes and cause me to see, understand, and walk in my purpose. Show me the steps I need to take so I don't waste time. Open my heart to the Father's counsel. Help me discover my purpose, to live a fulfilled, abundant life, and not miss out on what Abba Father has for me.

Don't Isolate. Know That You Are Not Alone

One of the worst feelings to have is that you are by yourself. But you are never alone.

> Let your conversation be without covetousness; and be content with such things as ye have: for he hath said, I will never leave thee, nor forsake thee. (Hebrews 13:5)

> Teaching them to observe all things whatsoever I have commanded you: and, lo, I am with you always, even unto the end of the world. Amen. (Matthew 28:20)

There are many reasons why we feel alone. Perhaps when we needed assistance in a difficult time, those we looked to for help weren't there; or maybe we were struggling within our heart with a challenge, but no one seemed to understand what we were going through. You must know that God is always with you in the darkest and most difficult moments. When my mother died, I felt so alone. I felt God let me down because He didn't heal her after we had prayed for years. I was miserable, restless, and heartbroken. There was such an empty feeling in my heart. Every day, I cried and asked God to help me and heal my broken heart (even though I was upset with Him). Thank God for those who prayed for me during that time. I don't know how I would have made it through that season. God heard my prayer and the prayers of His intercessors, and rescued me. I began to gradually feel the burden lift and my faith being restored. It was an inner healing process. I never felt so alone. I want you to know that even if you don't feel God and you are upset with Him, He will not leave you alone. He will rescue you, just like He rescued me.

In order to walk in boldness in this new era, we must be persuaded that God is with us. Even when we don't understand the rejection, pain, tribulation, or challenge, we have a loving heavenly Father, an advocate (Jesus), and the Holy Spirit living in us to help us overcome. Knowing that God is with you when you are in the lowest, darkest valley will keep you moving forward during challenging times. Don't be afraid to ask for prayer and help. We've all been through situations that caused us to feel alone. We need each other. When God created Adam, He said it is not good for man to be alone, so He created a helper for him. God knew Adam needed someone to talk to and laugh with. He needed someone to share his thoughts with. Our eternal God is with us and knows that we need others in our lives to help us. You are not an island. God sees you and knows how to change the dynamics and provide help every time. Put your trust in our God, Who created us, and be confident that He knows how we feel, knows what we need, and will come through every time.

> And the Lord God said, it is not good that the man should be alone; I will make him an help meet for him. (Genesis 2:18)

Army Workout Exercises

1. What are you called to do? What are you doing about it?
2. What are you passionate about?
3. Write a personal mission statement.

Reflective Moments & Assignments

Recall when Jesus saved you. Give Him praise.

Write your testimony and share it (as much as you can) with someone who doesn't know Jesus as their Lord and Savior.

Make a list of three people who will pray with you this week. Contact them and set aside time to pray with them.

CHAPTER 3

PRAY AND BELIEVE THAT GOD HEARS YOUR PRAYERS

And this is the confidence that we have in him, that, if we ask any thing according to his will, he heareth us: And if we know that he hears us, whatsoever we ask, we know that we have the petitions that we desired of him. (1 John 5:14–15)

We must realize the access and influence we have as believers in Jesus Christ. The God of the universe, Who created the sun, moon, stars, and everything that exists, hears your prayer. Yes. He hears you. To be a successful warrior, it's essential to know that God hears you.

Prayer is communication between you and God. It is a relationship experience that occurs when you share what's on your heart with the Lord, and He shares His heart with you. Prayer is not a religious obligation, but a commitment to maintain a relationship with the one you love. Relationships do not last long without communication. When communication is missing, assumptions are made, and conflicting thoughts can develop.

In prayer, there is an exchange. You speak to God, and He speaks to you. You must learn to spend time listening to the Lord. When you pray, expect to hear from Him. He has ears and is attentive to you. Wait patiently for the Holy Spirit to reveal His heart and give you guidance and assurance. Don't allow your intellect to be a stumbling block, and be open to kingdom communication and sounds. Ask the Holy Spirit to remove the barriers of religious mindsets, rhetoric, and anything that blocks your ears from hearing God's strategic insight. You must hear from our heavenly Father to move succinctly with His plan. A consistent prayer life will season you with grace, discernment, humility, and love.

There were times when I would pray about someone I was upset with and tell God all the things she or he did to me. After I vented, God didn't seem surprised or upset with the person I was talking to Him about. He focused on my heart and caused me to look at myself. When I examined myself, I realized how much forgiveness and mercy He granted me; I left that time of prayer refreshed, encouraged, and most of all free. We can leave prayer and devotion bound if we don't allow the love of God to free us from our own biases. Many times, we want God to get the people who hurt us and love to quote the scripture;

"they will reap what they have sown." Let's change our prayer language and ask God to free the people who hurt us, so they don't hurt anyone else. Let's stop desiring for them to reap heartache and pain; instead, let's pray that they experience the healing and love of God and be a blessing in His Kingdom. Imagine if we reaped all the stuff we have sown? I wouldn't be alive. Thank God for His mercy and forgiveness in our lives. I believe prayer changes things, but most of all, I know that prayer changes me.

"Cast all your cares on him for He cares for you" (1 Peter 5:7). Share all your heart with God. He is listening and will respond. God loves for you to talk to Him, and He loves to communicate to you. Imagine being in a relationship with someone and never talking to them? God wants to hear from you. It is so important to include God in every area of your life. I remember praying and asking God to send me the husband He desired for me. I believed God knew what I needed, and He sent Cy, who has been my husband for thirty-five years. Cy is the funniest and most joyful person I know. He loves God and has a heart for people. Just like every marriage, we have had challenges and rough times, but through it all, God has kept us, and we are still in love and best friends.

I also prayed and asked God to give us twins and a son. I've always wanted children, and I made my petition to God. I also shared my desires with close friends, who came into agreement with me for the prayer request. After I got pregnant, my dear friend prophesied that I was going to have twins. I was so excited, but when I had my sonogram, the doctor told me it was only one baby. When I got home, I called my friend and told her that the sonogram showed only one baby. She replied in a soft, confident voice; I heard the Lord say "twins". She didn't back down from her conviction. She remained confident and assured that she gave me the Word of God. I was determined to thank God for the baby in my womb, and I worshipped Him throughout the entire pregnancy. On October 11, 1989, God blessed us with a son. Jordan was a handsome and hefty eight-pound baby. Never forget that God's ways are perfect towards you. God answered my prayer in His divine order. (Psalm 18:30)

Two years after Jordan was born, I was pregnant again. I had another sonogram, and the doctor told me, "Mrs. Gaffney, you are having twins."

I started rejoicing and heard God say to me, "Because you worshipped me for the nine months when you didn't get the twins first, I want you to know that I haven't forgotten you."

On August 11, 1992, Ramah and Moriah were born. Ramah was seven pounds, and Moriah was eight pounds. With God's strength and great mercy, I delivered two healthy, beautiful twin girls. I was overjoyed.

God hears and answers prayers. Trust His answers to your prayers. He is already in your future and knows what is best. Just praise Him! Learn to praise God when things don't line up exactly the way you wanted. Praise Him! Praise Him in your storm. Praise Him in the valley. Praise Him on the mountain. Giving God praise when you can't see your way requires faith in His word. Your praise in the middle of the battle is making a declaration that you trust Jesus more than what you see or feel. God knows what is best for you. Wait patiently for Him to show you His infallible results. He is faithful to us. He will not fail you.

Prayer is a key to spiritual growth and success. It prepares you for the present and the future. Let prayer be a lifestyle. Here are a few recommendations to help you deal with the challenges and walk in God's strategy:

1. Pray first thing in the morning, before you begin the day.
2. Spend time praising God for what He has already done.
3. Remember, God loves for you to talk to Him. Include Him in your thoughts, and He will help you make wise decisions.
4. Study His Word to know His heart. Listen to His heart and obey His instructions.
5. Expect direction, insight, healing, and hope.
6. Pray throughout the day.
7. Be confident, and know that God hears you.

Prayer for Awareness

Holy Spirit, help me pray. Cause my heart to be sensitive to you and expose all selfish agendas. Use me as an effective intercessor to bring glory to God. Open my eyes, Holy Spirit, so I can see things the way God wants me to see them.

Testimony and Reflection

After my dad passed, my mom came to live with us. My sister Karen (who lived close by), and I became her primary caretakers. Caring for mom wasn't an easy job; she was such a strong woman of God and one who led by example. She lived an honorable life, and the memories I have of her are filled with love and gratitude.

As I was planning to attend my niece's wedding, I secretly prayed that God would heal my mother so she could attend the ceremony. That didn't happen, but Charissa and Joshua had the most beautiful wedding celebration. At the reception, we sat down with my brother Brian, his wife, and their children. Just as we took our seats, my sister-in-law informed us that a table had already been reserved for us. We moved to that table, which had been decorated with family memorabilia. As I sat down, right in front of me was a picture of my mom, with her big gracious smile.

The Spirit of God said to me, "I heard your prayers."

Even though my mother couldn't attend the wedding, her picture spoke volumes to my heart. It was a reminder of her loving and gracious heart. God wanted me to see my mother as I knew her; strong, bold and vibrant. It was a divine setup. God knows what is best, and He heard my prayers. Even though I couldn't understand everything at that time, and even now I still ask Him about it, I know that God has my mother and has always taken care of her.

Never underestimate the power of your prayers. God hears them, no matter how small or big. He cares for you with an unrelenting love and will be with you through all of life's challenges to remind you of His faithfulness.

Army Workout Exercises

1. Have a praise party. Start praising God for all the things He has done and will do for you.
2. Invite the Holy Spirit to help you pray the heart of Jesus. Expect results.
3. Evaluate and describe your prayer life.
4. Is your prayer life effective? Why (or why not)? If yes, discuss the results.
5. List three scriptures that are examples of the power of prayer.

CHAPTER 4

DEPEND ON THE HOLY SPIRIT'S GUIDANCE

Howbeit, when he, the Spirit of truth comes He will
guide you into all truth for he shall not speak of
himself but whatsoever he shall hear, that shall he
speak, and he will show you things to come.
—John 16:13

God is truth. We must trust everything in His Word.

> Jesus saith unto him, I am the way, the truth,
> and the life: no man cometh unto the Father,
> but by me. (John 14:6)

When you are born again, it is imperative to
learn how to live a spirit-led life. God gave
us the Holy Spirit to help us understand the
supernatural life. The spirit-led life is totally

opposite from the natural life. To be successful in the spirit-led life, you must have a trainer who will teach you how to operate in your new space. The Holy Spirit is the trainer who reveals the heart and plan of God for your life. The carnal life is enmity with God; it cannot understand His way. In other words, we won't know how to experience the purpose God has planned for our lives without the Holy Spirit, who is the Spirit of truth. God has promised us a Comforter to help us navigate through this life. The Holy Spirit, Who dwells in us, is obligated to lead us into all truth. We must allow His leadership to orchestrate our steps. Deception is raging, and those who don't depend on the guidance of the Holy Spirit will be led down the wrong path.

The world should see believers radiating like bright lights, leading the way to Jesus in love. We cannot afford to be led by our motives or emotions. The Holy Spirit will lead us in truth, to the truth, and reveal the truth. He will show us things to come. The Holy Spirit will reveal the mind of our heavenly Father. Yes, we can know the mind of God, the Creator of the universe, the One Who created us for His glory. Imagine driving down a road in a new city and not knowing where to go. What would you do? Well, of course, with today's technology, you can use the GPS on your cell phone. The navigation service will take you to your desired destination. The Holy Spirit is our GPS. He will show us the right road to take all the time. He doesn't lose power or direction because of problems with the weather or a satellite. He is sent from God to assist us in life.

We think we know how to live but without God's directives we are lost. The Holy Spirit has a customized plan for your life, and it's important to know the destiny God has planned. God knows the way we need to take and has given us the Holy Spirit to show us. We cannot minimize the power of the Holy Spirit. The Holy Spirit makes us aware of what's happening in the earth realm and in the heavens. He will cause us to see things that we cannot see with our natural eyes. The Holy Spirit will supernaturally open our inner ear to hear sounds that are not normally heard. He will use natural things to awaken us to what is going on in the heavens. We must live a Holy Spirit-led life to enjoy the treasures God has for us.

We have adapted to the normal way of life. We go to school or work, spend time with family or friends, eat, sleep, and get up the next day to follow the same routine. With the Holy Spirit, we are immersed in a journey of exploration, discovery, and kingdom illumination. Pause for one moment, and ask the Holy Spirit to take over, to place your life on the divine trajectory God has ordained for it. No longer accept a robotic, mundane, predictable life. Ask the Holy Spirit to baptize you afresh with fire, love, and the power of our resurrected King, Jesus.

Expect to walk differently now. Rely on the Holy Spirit's leadership, and trust Him to take you places you've never been. God wants His people to depend on the Comforter and walk in power. It is time for us to arise, awaken, and ascend into kingdom authority and influence our world. This world needs you to walk in the Spirit. The only way to fulfill your purpose is through the guidance of the Holy Spirit. He knows the roads, highways, and best travel routes to take you. Holy Spirit will show you things you've never seen or even thought about.

Many spirits are operating in this world, and they are not holy. Living inside of you is the Spirit of truth. Move pass religious thoughts, and put your expectancy in the power of

God, manifested through His spirit operating
in you.

Army Workout Exercises

1. How can a person grieve the Holy Spirit?
2. List three ways you can depend on the Holy Spirit more.
3. What type of personality does the Holy Spirit have?
4. How is the Holy Spirit leading your life?

Study the Word of God

Study to show yourself approved unto to God; a workman
needeth not to be ashamed rightly dividing the world of truth.
—2 Timothy 2:15

The soldier who doesn't know how to use his weapons will
not be able to fight. We must be adept in God's word, which is
our sword. Studying the word prepares us for the challenges of
life, spiritual warfare, to win souls, and in understanding our
purpose.

We will not survive these Roaring Twenties and beyond without
reading, studying, applying, and meditating on the Word of
God. Reading and studying are two different applications. You
can read something but not study it. Study is the devotion of
time and attention to acquiring knowledge on a particular
subject, especially by means of books. Reading is a skill that one

uses to review, scan, and interpret text. The Word of God gives us an understanding of the Lord's will. How can we progress in this world without knowing the mind of God?

The Word of God gives us the ability to discern, which is the process of determining God's desire in a situation or identifying the true nature of a thing, such as assessing whether something is good or evil. From birth, we are taught to use our natural senses to make decisions; tasting, touching, hearing, and seeing are what we use to guide us. These senses are given to us by God and are a blessing to help us navigate in the natural realm. God's Word trains and guides us beyond our natural senses.

God's Word opens our understanding to the supernatural power, purpose, and plan of God and helps us make fruitful choices. It is time to make sound decisions that produce results. Aren't you tired of making decisions that are ineffective? Doesn't it bother you when you see the same cycles, poor relationships, difficult financial conditions, and lack of spiritual maturity, year after year, because of the same bad decisions? We can no longer stay in cycles that oppress our purpose. This era requires cycles to be broken so we don't sabotage God's blessings.

Take a moment to reflect over your life. It takes prayer coupled with faith in God's word to break cycles. Studying the Word of God and having faith in the Word will give you the stamina and strength to see the tactics of the devil and also see your own flesh. The Word is a supernatural mirror. You will see yourself and what needs to be done to stop generational cycles.

JUDITH GAFFNEY

Diligently applying the principles of the Word will destroy cycles. The Word brings enlightenment and inspiration. We should not read the Word as an everyday story but study it to discover the treasures of God.

God's Word is a map that tells us which way to go and how to act when we get there. For example, the Word of God tells us to love our enemies and bless those who persecute us and use us: "But I say unto you, love your enemies, bless them that curse you, do good to them that hate you, and pray for them which despitefully use you, and persecute you" (Matthew 5:44).

As we move into positions of influence to impact our world, the enemy will intensify his tactics to discourage us, deceive us, and deploy arsenals of distraction. We must know how to bless those the enemy is using and sincerely pray for their deliverance. To sincerely pray for your enemy is a sign of growth and maturity that only comes with having faith and studying the Word of God. When was the last time you prayed for your enemies?

The enemy wants us to think that studying the Word of God is boring. Always remember that the devil is a liar and the father of lies. Everything he says is a lie. God's Word is not superficial. His Word delves into the core of our existence and transforms the mind to align with a divine perspective. God's Word is life; and is alive. His Word will heal a broken heart and put you on a faith journey that is overshadowed with peace. God's Word will give you counsel and direction. Psalm 119 is filled with declarations about the power of God's Word.

God's Word is the sustainer of our lives. We must "eat and digest" the Word daily and allow the Word to purify our mind from the world's influence. Psalm 119:9 says, "Wherewithal shall a young man cleanse his way? By taking heed thereto according to thy word."

Every soldier engaged in war must be equipped with the correct gear. Soldiers are protected by their gear. We are in a spiritual battle against principalities and powers we can't see. When I think about the Covid-19 pandemic, which has taken so many lives, it is something we cannot see, but we must take the necessary precautions to stop it from spreading. Some of those precautions are wearing masks, washing our hands, and keeping a six-foot distance. To war against the powers of darkness, there are measures Christians must take to experience victory. First, we must put on the entire armor, and part of the armor is the sword of the spirit, which is the Word of God. How can we use this weaponry if we don't study it? The Word of God will make us sharp, keen, and prepared to handle what we can't see. We are liberated through the Word. The sword of the spirit severs the cords of toxicity that have been wrapped around our minds and frees us to walk in confidence, power, and authority.

> Put on the whole armour of God, that ye may
> be able to stand against the wiles of the devil.

JUDITH GAFFNEY

For we wrestle not against flesh and blood, but against principalities, against powers, against the rulers of the darkness of this world, against spiritual wickedness in high places.

Wherefore take unto you the whole armour of God, that ye may be able to withstand in the evil day, and having done all, to stand.

Stand therefore, having your loins girt about with truth, and having on the breastplate of righteousness;

And your feet shod with the preparation of the gospel of peace;

Above all, taking the shield of faith, wherewith ye shall be able to quench all the fiery darts of the wicked.

And take the helmet of salvation, and the sword of the Spirit, which is the word of God. (Ephesians 6:11–17)

What you eat can determine how healthy you are now and in the future. Did you sit down at the table today and get nourished by the Word of God?

Army Workout Exercises

1. List three scriptures that speak about your spiritual health.
2. Write a recipe for good success using the Word of God.
3. List three scriptures you could use to bring someone to Jesus.
4. How do you know you are saved? List three scriptures.

Prayer: Father, in the name of Jesus, thank you for your Word! It is filled with promises and instructions for me to live by. I receive everything you have for me in your Word and delight in knowing that you are a covenant keeper.

CHAPTER 5

THE FUNDAMENTALS

Have a heart to serve others; do not be selfish.

> For, brethren, ye have been called unto liberty;
> only use not liberty for an occasion to the flesh,
> but by love serve one another. (Galatians 5:13)

Be aware of your motives and make sure you serve others with pure intentions. Love is not boastful! Love is considerate and kind.

It is so easy to become self-consumed. We live in a world that encourages us to be self-centered; a world filled with "do me" attitude. Let's not get it twisted. Self-care and self-love are important. The Bible states that we must love others as we love ourselves. You can't love others if you don't appreciate and love who God has created you to be. However, the worldly mindset promotes an egotistical view of one as supreme and better than others.

This perspective is filled with arrogance, pride, and selfishness. One day during a meeting at my job, I was jotting down notes, and the Holy Spirit convicted me and spoke to my heart and said, "Write it neater."

In my mind, I responded, *What's wrong with it? I can read it.*

After my reply, I received a rebuke that revealed the heart of God. The Holy Spirit spoke to me and said, "That's the problem: you can read it. It's all about you. What about someone else who may need to read the instructions in your notes? They might have difficulty reading it, so make it clear for them."

This experience was an eye-opener for me. I began to really understand God's love. He wanted me to write neater for others, including myself, but I was so stuck on me. Have you ever been there? I asked God to forgive me for being so self-centered and to help me change. Thankfully, the Holy Spirit deals with every area of our lives.

Love reminds us to serve, even when it is not convenient or popular. Serving others requires us to die out to selfish agendas. If we don't serve with humility and love, it is futile. Authentic servitude is a supernatural action that brings godly results. When you serve from the heart, it is unto God and not for the approval of others. I am not saying this is an easy action, but it is a necessary one.

Romans 8:19 declares, "For the earnest expectation of the creature waiteth for the manifestation of the sons of God." The world is waiting for the manifestation of the sons of God. This scripture is exhorting Christians to take their place in love and humility; to live a life representing God's light in a dark world. The world needs to see true love. They are searching for love in all the wrong places, and Christians, by the power of the Holy Spirit, are the only people on the planet who can show the love of Jesus.

How can we do this? By submitting ourselves to Jesus and allowing the Holy Spirit to love through us. Have you asked the Holy Spirit to love through you? Ask Him now to baptize you afresh in His love and to help you to let Him love through you.

I recall when a minister offended me deeply; I didn't want to forgive them from my heart. When I saw them ministering, I was angry and didn't want to listen. Have you ever felt that way? Grinning, smiling, and saying, "Praise the Lord," while wishing a certain person wasn't in your company. The Holy Spirit dealt with my offended heart and revealed God's relentless mercy, forgiveness, and love over my life. With God's help, I was able to genuinely release the offense and enjoy the ministry of the person who hurt me.

How will the world see Jesus if we don't walk in the light of His counsel? How will they experience love that is pure if we don't show love for one another? It's time to get off the lazy chair and serve one another in love. Let's make sure that God's agenda is in our heart.

We are the sons of God because His seed, the incorruptible Word of God, lives in us. 1 Peter 1:23 says, "Being born again, not of corruptible seed, but of incorruptible, by the word of God, which liveth and abideth for ever." Hope resides in us and all the keys to abundant life. Jesus saved us, and now we are born again. 1 John 3:2 says, "Beloved, now are we the sons of God, and it doth not yet appear what we shall be: but we know that, when he shall appear, we shall be like him; for we shall see him as he is."

Remember and reflect on the heart of Jesus. Luke 19:10 says, "For the Son of man is come to seek and to save that which was lost." Jesus is always about changing the lives of others. His first miracle was at a wedding when they ran out of wine, and He turned the water into wine. He wants to be invited and included at every event. He turned the water into wine to be a blessing to the married couple and their guests at the wedding feast. The master of the feast told the bridegroom that at weddings, they set out the premium wine first, and when men are well drunk, then they serve the lesser quality. But at this wedding, Jesus changed the outcome.. . He wants us to always serve the best and be the best servers. He changed the dynamics at the wedding and brought the solution.

With Christ in us, the hope of glory, we carry solutions to change lives, events, situations, and circumstances. Let's ask God every day to use our lives to bring hope and solutions. We are called to serve others. Does that mean you are not a leader? Of course not. True leaders know how to serve others and ask God for the solution. Our world lacks true leadership. We serve the world with the love of Jesus by how we treat one another, how we treat the unsaved, what we say, and our actions. The world must hear the Word of God from Christians; we must show it to them. We must tell them Jesus is the way, the truth, and the life. Tell people that Jesus has plans for their lives and loves them more than they can imagine.

Arise soldier and walk boldly in love with your spiritual army gear on. Be strong and stand secure with the "blessed assurance" that Jesus lives and reigns in your heart! Don't be ashamed of who you are. Our Heavenly Father has His hands on you. You are called and chosen by Him.

I was a member of a social media chat group that was started by the students who were in a course I took at FIT (Fashion Institute of Technology). In the beginning of the Covid-19 pandemic, when New York was the epicenter, there was an urgent request listed in the FIT chat group for someone to make additional PPE for the ICU nurses at Columbia Presbyterian Hospital in Manhattan. They needed scrub caps to protect their hair as they treated patients with the virus.

I reached out to the ICU nurse who sent the message, and she explained that they had a shortage of PPE gear to protect their hair. God put a passion in my heart to help these ICU nurses who were working tirelessly; day and night, to save lives. I shared the situation with the ministry, and many of them donated money to help me get the scrub caps made. I also shared my idea with my seamstress, Mrs. Ray, and like a trooper, she sewed all the scrub caps to meet the needs of these essential workers. I thank God for her; God wants us to know how to partner with others to serve the world so they can see a demonstration of His love.

Army Workout Exercises

1. List three ways you can be a better servant.
2. List and discuss three scriptures that discuss servanthood.
3. Discuss and define servant leadership.
4. Give three examples of biblical personalities who were models of good servants.
5. Exercise your faith and step out in new ways to help others deal with their challenges.

Fasting

Howbeit this kind goeth not out but by prayer and fasting.
—Matthew 17:21

We must be ready to fast and pray. Fasting is not trying to get God to do something for you. He has already done everything. Jesus said it is finished. God has done it. We are free; we're delivered; we have the greatest love, peace, and joy. We have the Holy Spirit living in us to lead us and guide us into all truth. We are complete in Him in whom the fullness of the Godhead dwells bodily. It's time to really walk in it.

> For in him dwelleth all the fulness of the Godhead bodily. And ye are complete in him, which is the head of all principality and power. (Colossians 2:9–10)

We have been redeemed; we are children of God. Everything we need is in Jesus. Jesus paid it all. Therefore, fasting benefits you. It helps you to silence the noise of the flesh and opens your spirit to the sound of God's heartbeat. Fasting sensitizes you to the spirit realm and allows you to hear what God is saying more clearly. Fasting is also good for our natural bodies because it facilitates detoxification. Our bodies need a break from the daily intake of sugar, caffeine, and fatty foods. Fasting purifies our body's system and facilitates healing. The results from fasting are beneficial, spiritually and naturally. If you are on medication or under a doctor's care, consult with your physician to determine the type of fast that is best for you.

Most importantly, fasting must be coupled with prayer. If not, you will be aligning with the world's view. Fasting is a common practice by people from different religions. One definition for fasting is, a practice that has been associated with a wide array of potential health benefits, including weight loss, as well as improved blood sugar control, heart health, brain function, and cancer prevention. As we can see, people fast for different reasons. God's army must fast with a heavenly agenda that has been given to us by the Holy Spirit. We fast for a purpose and expect supernatural results.

When you fast, write down a prayer focus and stick with it. James 4:3 says, "Ye ask, and receive not, because ye ask amiss, that ye may consume it upon your lusts." In 2020, during the Covid-19 pandemic, God gave our ministry specific points to pray. Every day throughout the year, at specific times, we came together on a conference call and prayed God's agenda. When you are fasting, make sure it is God's agenda and not yours. Isaiah 58:6 says, "It is not the fast that I have chosen: To loose the bands of wickedness, undo heavy burdens, let the oppressed go free, and to break every yoke?" This scripture shows us the heart of God; it's why we should proclaim a fast. Fasting should always be about God's heart. When you fast, you are not trying to move God's hand. It's about hearing the pulse of His heart and moving succinctly with Him.

God has given us authority in the earth, and fasting is part of His arsenal. Spend time praying for a specific region, person, or circumstance. God's reward is speedily realized in fasting because our eyes are open to His realm and sound. This allows us to hear strategic plans from the councils of heaven. We must make room in our lifestyle for prayer and fasting.

If you have never fasted before, start off by missing one meal, and then the next time, two meals. Be persistent. Even if you mess up and don't accomplish the complete fast, try again. Never give up. Ask the Holy Spirit to help you fast and to keep you during the fast. Fasting will benefit your soul. There were times during a fast that I could sense the presence of God dealing with my thoughts and enlightening my heart to His counsel. Sometimes, we don't realize the emotional baggage we carry. Fasting and prayer facilitate baggage removal. God can show us ourselves when we are still and wait in His presence. Life is often filled with hustle and bustle; many times, we miss instructions because we are so used to getting up and going. Fasting and prayer allows you to be still and hear the voice of God. I recommend that when you are fasting and praying, turn off the TV, minimize the phone calls, and curtail social media engagement. Worship God, seek His direction, and ask for His solutions. I believe that what God can do for us with one moment in His presence, we couldn't do for ourselves in a lifetime. We need God's heart and should take time out to be quiet, listen, and let the Holy Spirit renew us.

In the book of Esther, the Jews were going to be destroyed because of the evil plot devised by Haman. Mordecai, Esther's close relative, sought her help. Esther called for a fast for three days, and God spared the Jewish nation. The fast changed history. The plot was destroyed, and God's people were promoted and honored. Can you imagine? An entire nation was going to be annihilated because of a sinister plot, and God overturned the plot. God hears the cry of His people and will change history to preserve them. Fasting will bring results. It is a supernatural weapon that opens your ears and eyes.

> Go, gather together all the Jews that are present in Shushan, and fast ye for me, and neither eat nor drink three days, night or day: I also and my maidens will fast likewise; and so will I go in unto the king, which is not according to the law: and if I perish, I perish. (Esther 4:16)

Fast for a cause. Don't fast with carnal intentions. Spend time praying and fasting for others, and God will cause great things to happen for you. Whatever you do in secret for others unto God, He sees it and will reward you. God's reward is eternal and priceless. The reward from men is temporal and will fade. Honor God in your fast. Make it a time of intimacy, and when the fast is completed, you will be refreshed and transformed.

Rest: Rely, Endure, Stand, and Trust

> There remaineth therefore a rest to the people of God. For he that is entered into his rest, he also hath ceased from his own works, as God did from his.
> —Hebrews 4:9–10

To be an effective warrior in God's army, you must know how to rest naturally and spiritually. If you don't rest, the cares of life and dealing with the principalities in this age will wear you out. You will feel drained and lose stamina. Rest is important for your body and spirit. Rest has been shown to improve cardiovascular health and lower blood pressure and cortisol levels. Sleeping doesn't mean resting. Resting occurs when you are still, physically and mentally. It is a cease of movement. When you get good rest, you feel refreshed and renewed. You are ready to take on new tasks or complete old tasks. Rest helps you get ready for the challenges, assignments, and daily routines of life. It is so important to make sure your natural body gets rest so you can work with God to fulfill His desire for your life.

It is a horrible feeling when you have work to do and feel tired. When you are tired, it's difficult to focus and be your best. God wants your best, and in order to give Him that, you must learn to rest. Spiritual rest is ceasing from the works of the flesh and depending on God. "Ceasing from the works of the flesh" means that you no longer are depending upon yourself. You have matured and come to the realization that flesh, or the carnal nature, is enmity with God and cannot bring spiritual results.

Rest is knowing that by God's grace, you are saved through faith, not of yourself. There is nothing you can do to earn salvation or the mercy of God. Jesus died and rose again so you could be saved and live with Him forever. You must accept the work that Jesus has done for you by faith. Rest is trusting in the finished work of Jesus and knowing that the price has already been paid for you to have success in every area of your life. A rested warrior is one who is confident, stable, and prepared. When the enemy brings thoughts of fear, doubt, and confusion to rested warriors, they are ready to pull out the sword, which is the Word of God, and slay the injustices that wage war on their mind. With the Holy Spirit's assistance, rested warriors take captive their thoughts and bring them into submission to the lordship of Christ. This is not an easy action. It requires determination and persistence. Don't give up. Make a conscious effort to submit your thoughts to Jesus and then rest, knowing He is faithful. Ask the Holy Spirit to help you.

> Casting down imaginations, and every high thing that exalts itself against the knowledge of God, and bringing into captivity every thought to the obedience of Christ. (2 Corinthians 10:5)

If you don't rest, you can't dream. You were created to have big dreams.

Rely

Relying on God is realizing that you need Him to live and that you cannot survive without Him. It is asking Him for direction and trusting that He will lead you the right way. Have you ever been in a situation when there was a problem that seemed unsurmountable? Jesus is the solution to every problem; He will give you the specificity that is needed. You must fully depend on God's Word and not have faith in the systems of this world. Every system will fail, but God cannot fail you and will never fail you. How can you live in a world governed by fleshy and demonic influences? By relying on God and His Spirit to guide you. When you rely on the promises of God, you can rest.

> And let us not be weary in well doing: for in due season we shall reap, if we faint not. (Galatians 6:9)

Endure

> Thou therefore endure hardness, as a
> good soldier of Jesus Christ.
> —2 Timothy 2:3

Paul encourages Timothy to endure hardships, like a good soldier of Jesus Christ. As the demonic realm increases its evil activity, bringing deception and chaos, the church must know how to endure hard times and handle them. Endurance is the ability to go through prolonged trials without giving up. God's sufficient grace will help us endure hardships. It is important to keep communicating with Jesus during hardship and praise Him for what He has already done. We must also learn to listen to God so we can apprehend His plan.

While you are going through difficult times, make a conscious effort to thank God for His faithfulness to you. Spend time reflecting over your life, and write down at least three major things the Lord did for you. Praise God for what He did. Never forget that Jesus is the same today, yesterday, and forever. What He did in your yesterday, He can do again tomorrow. He will not leave you in the fiery furnace. God specializes in bringing His people out. He brought the children of Israel out of Egypt with His own hand and destroyed their enemy right before their eyes. He is sovereign, and His timing is perfect. I have discovered that praying diligently, asking others to pray for me, and meditating on His Word has helped me endure difficult seasons in life.

Stand

> Wherefore take unto you the whole armour of
> God, that ye may be able to withstand in the
> evil day, and having done all, to stand.
> —Ephesians 6:13

With their whole armor on, God's army must stand tall and not be intimidated by the news or other reports that are sent to shake their faith. There will always be wars, rumors of wars, and catastrophic events until Jesus returns and establishes His kingdom. Are we prepared? Standing is the act of maintaining an upright posture. Our posture must be one with confidence and assurance that God is with us.

The world is dark and getting darker. People are looking for answers. How will they find us if we are sitting in fear and despair? We must stand on the Word of God as those He has called and commissioned for such a time as this. God has equipped us to stand.

I remember when my mother was hospitalized. The doctor spoke to me about her condition and concluded with: "You can just let her die in peace, or we can be aggressive and treat her." I was so nervous that my legs and stomach felt weak. Even though things didn't look good medically, God put it in my spirit not to give up. He encouraged me to stand in His Word and speak life to my mother. I decided to stand even when my natural body was giving in to fear. It wasn't easy, but God helped me through it. I told the doctors that I wanted them to be aggressive with her treatment and do whatever was necessary to improve her quality of life. My mother lived another eight years. We must stand while looking to God for divine assistance. His way will always bring the best outcome.

Trust

> Blessed is the man that trusteth in the
> Lord, and whose hope the Lord is.
> —Jeremiah 17:7

Trusting in God produces the rewards of contentment and peace. *Blessed* means "happy." True happiness begins with trust in God. We are happy when our trust is in the Lord. He is immortal, invisible, omnipotent; He lives and reigns forever. He created everything, and everything must respond to His voice. When we fully trust in God, we know that our lives are under His care and protection, and He will make sure that all things will work out for our good and His glory.

Authentic relationships are built on trust, and Jesus desires relationship. He wants us to know that we can trust Him with our life. People, governments, and all the structures of the world will fail, but Jesus will not; He is infinite. He is the only eternal, firm foundation. In Daniel chapter 3, Daniel's three friends were going to be thrown into a fiery furnace because they wouldn't bow down and worship King Nebuchadnezzar's idol. They trusted God with their lives and didn't succumb to the threat of death. They said with bold confidence that God would deliver them, and even if He didn't deliver them, that He was still able. This is an example of complete trust.

God's army must be ready to go through fiery trials and trust the Lord's outcome. There will be times when we will be asked to do certain things or go certain places that God has warned us not to. Our jobs might be threatened, our relationships, even our lives. We must trust that God's way is the path we need to take. After the three Hebrew boys were bound and thrown into the fiery furnace, the king looked inside and saw a fourth man in the furnace with them. The king was astonished because the three young men were not consumed; they were untied, and some unknown man was walking with them. God will be with

His army in the most difficult times; He'll make sure when we come out of the situation that we won't look like what we have been through. God's army will go through persecutions so the world can see He is sovereign and has the final say over death and life.

Army Workout Exercises

1. List three Bible figures who had to trust God. Discuss their challenges and how they dealt with them.
2. Write a brief testimony about a situation in your life when you found it difficult to trust God.
3. List and discuss three scriptures about trusting God.

Take Care of Yourself

> Beloved, I wish above all things that thou mayest prosper and be in health, even as thy soul prospereth.
> —3 John 1:2

Due to our busy lives, we often neglect to take care of our physical and emotional health. It is important to love yourself enough that you take care of your body and mind. Our bodies are the temple of God, and His spirit lives in us. If we don't take care of our body, it will deteriorate. The body is mortal and will return to the dust. However, our spirit needs a body to live in to accomplish the will of God on earth. If our body or mind is not well, it can be very difficult to execute the will of God. If God has called you to be a doctor, engineer, missionary, or lawyer, how can you assist others if you don't feel well or think well? Self-care is not carnal or fleshy; it is the will of God.

Army of God, try to exercise daily, eat a well-balanced nutritional diet, and stay away from refined sugars. Take care of yourself emotionally, and don't worry about being everything to everyone; that's God's responsibility. Let God be Who He is. He is a Savior, deliverer, friend closer than a brother, mother, father, companion, the lifter of our head, our redeemer, and way-maker. We should be there for our family and friends, but we must let God be their salvation.

Here are some suggestions for taking care of yourself emotionally:

1. Pray to God and ask Him to help you overcome your hurts.
2. Deal with your pain, layer by layer. Allow the healing process to begin.
3. Don't be afraid to get professional counseling or ask for help.
4. Stay away from toxic relationships.
5. Learn to forgive. You will free yourself.
6. Be honest and real about your situation. Search God's word and apply God's principles to your life.
7. Don't be scared to deal with the thoughts that bother you.
8. Surround yourself with those who genuinely care about your well-being and will pray with you.

Many believers face mental battles and are afraid to deal with them. God wants you healthy in your mind; sometimes, healing is a process. Confront your mental battles, expose them, and get help when you need it. If you don't, your relationships, dreams, and visions will be sabotaged and go unrealized. God wants you to experience His liberty to dream and think, which is priceless. Don't allow the hurt from your past to rob your future aspirations and dreams.

Army Workout Exercises

1. Create a plan that will help you stay well physically and mentally. Include exercise, healthy relationships, and rest. Make sure to implement the plan. See attached schedules to help you record your accomplishments. Get an accountability partner to help you stay on track.
2. Discuss three biblical characters who overcame their pain and struggles.
3. Research and find scriptures about confronting and overcoming battles. Meditate on the scriptures and apply them.
4. Find three people in the bible who exhibited great strength and had healthy eating habits.

Fitness & Nutrition Schedule
Use this form to keep track of your exercise and nutrition.

	Sunday	Monday	Tuesday	Wednesday	Thursday	Friday	Saturday
Dates							
Warm Up Exercise(s)							
Daily Exercise(s)							
Breakfast							
Lunch							
Dinner							

JUDITH GAFFNEY

Mental Health Workout
Use this form to keep track of your progress.

	Sunday	Monday	Tuesday	Wednesday	Thursday	Friday	Saturday
Dates							
Talk To Jesus							
Find scriptures to encourage yourself							
Worship God							
Communicate/ Share							
Seek counsel							

THIRTY DAYS OF
BOOT CAMP

Take the challenge! Spend the next thirty days working out your spirit man. Take communion daily and thank God for the blood of Jesus Christ. Decree that the blood of Jesus has made you whole! Anoint your head with oil and make the declaration that you have the mind of Christ. You are preparing to strengthen your spiritual muscles. This plan is just to get you ready for a lifestyle change. Start off by praying these verses from the book of Ephesians:

> God of our Lord Jesus Christ, the Father of glory, give unto me the spirit of wisdom and revelation in the knowledge of him: Cause the eyes of my understanding to be enlightened; that I may know what is the hope of your calling, and what the riches of the glory of your inheritance in the saints, And what is the exceeding greatness of your power to me. For I believe in you Jesus. (Ephesians 1:17–19)

Day 1

Exercise your faith

> But without faith it is impossible to please him:
> for he that cometh to God must believe that
> he is, and that he is a rewarder of them that
> diligently seek him. (Hebrews 11:6)

Meditate on Hebrews 11:6. Ask Holy Spirit to help you to be a diligent seeker and know God as your rewarder. Walk in faith today. Write down three ways you walked in faith. Journal what Holy Spirit revealed to you. Journal how Holy Spirit assisted you.

Day 2

Be filled with hope

> Now the God of hope fill you with all joy and
> peace in believing, that ye may abound in hope,
> through the power of the Holy Ghost. (Romans
> 15:13)

Expect God to do exceedingly and abundantly above what you
ask or think. Praise Him for what He has done, and expect it
to happen. Look for it; He is the God of hope. Write down what
you are hoping for and pray this scripture: "God of hope fill me
with all joy and peace in believing, that I may abound in hope,
through the power of the Holy Ghost" (Romans 15:13).

Day 3

Know the greatness in you! Live great! Think great!

> Ye are of God, little children, and have overcome
> them: because greater is he that is in you, than
> he that is in the world. (1 John 4:4)

Walk in greatness. Believe what God's word says about you.
His word is truth. Ask Him to heal you from negative thoughts
and from words people have spoken that hurt you. Write three
scriptures that state what God says about you. Ask Holy Spirit
to help you walk in His greatness.

Day 4

Let God's peace rule

> And let the peace of God rule in your hearts, to
> the which also ye are called in one body; and be
> ye thankful. (Colossians 3:15)

The peace of God must rule in the warrior's heart. By allowing God's peace to have dominion in your heart, you will have the strength to overcome life's obstacles. Make up in your mind that His peace, which surpasses your understanding, will have the ultimate jurisdiction in your heart.

Day 5

You have the mind of Christ

> For who hath known the mind of the Lord, that
> he may instruct him? but we have the mind of
> Christ. (1 Corinthians 2:16)

You have the mind of Christ. Anoint your head today and decree, "I have the mind of Christ." Handle every challenge and situation with the mind of Christ.

Day 6

Let God's joy be in your life

> Thou wilt shew me the path of life: in thy
> presence is fulness of joy; at thy right hand there
> are pleasures for evermore. (Psalm 16:11)

Experience the joy of the Lord. Acknowledge the presence of
God, and thank Him for His joy, which will never run out.

Day 7

Be confident

> And this is the confidence that we have in him,
> that, if we ask any thing according to his will,
> he heareth us. (1 John 5:14)

Walk in confidence; God hears your prayers. Make sure that your prayer life is in alignment with the Word of God, and expect miracles.

Day 8

Trust the protection and power of God

> But thou, O LORD, art a shield for me; my glory,
> and the lifter up of mine head. (Psalm 3:3)

Know God as your shield today. Do not fear. God is greater and more powerful than anything seen or unseen. He is supernatural.

Day 9

Choose to worship Jesus in the midst of uncertainty

> O come, let us worship and bow down: let us
> kneel before the LORD our maker. (Psalm 95:6)

Make worship a lifestyle. Worship Jesus with all your heart.
Take time to soak in His presence.

Day 10

Be kind

> She openeth her mouth with wisdom; and in her
> tongue is the law of kindness. (Proverbs 31:26)

Kindness must be the law of your language. Call someone, and share a kind word today. Think kind thoughts about yourself and others. Be determined to not break the law of kindness.

Day 11

Let love reign

> Beloved, let us love one another: for love is of
> God; and everyone that loveth is born of God,
> and knoweth God. (1 John 4:7)

God is love, and we must love one another. Ask the Holy Spirit
to baptize you afresh in the love of God today. Ask Him to help
you walk in love.

Day 12

Let patience have its perfect work in you.

> But let patience have her perfect work, that ye
> may be perfect and entire, wanting nothing.
> (James 1:4)

Be patient with yourself and others. It takes time for a plant to grow. It requires water and sunlight. Allow the Holy Spirit to water and refresh your soul. Ask Him to help you walk in patience.

Day 13

Stand in the truth

> Stand therefore, having your loins girt about
> with truth, and having on the breastplate of
> righteousness. (Ephesians 6:14)

Stand in the truth and in righteousness. Do not lie to yourself.
Be truthful about yourself and with others. The truth will
liberate your soul.

Day 14

Be unmovable

> Therefore, my beloved brethren, be ye stedfast,
> unmoveable, always abounding in the work of
> the Lord, forasmuch as ye know that your labour
> is not in vain in the Lord. (1 Corinthians 15:58)

Do not be moved by the circumstances of life. Let your focus be on Jesus and His plan. Whatever you do unto God, it is not in vain. His reward is with you.

Day 15

Don't faint

> And let us not be weary in well doing for in
> due season we shall reap if we faint not.
> (Galatians 6:9)

Do not get weary while doing good things. One strategy of the enemy is to wear you down emotionally. He wants you to feel unappreciated, unloved, and unwanted. The enemy loves the spirit of rejection. God will never forget you, and He will cause you to reap the benefits of a great reward.

Day 16

Know God is sovereign

> The LORD shall reign forever, even thy God, O
> Zion, unto all generations. Praise ye the LORD.
> (Psalm 146:10)

Jesus reigns forever, and His kingdom has no end. Governments, people, businesses, and the systems of this world will fail. Jesus will never fail or falter. Celebrate today; you have the eternal Savior living in your heart.

Day 17

Shine bright today

> Ye are the light of the world. A city that is set on
> an hill cannot be hid. (Matthew 5:14)

Jesus has made us the light of the world. Know who you are,
and share the love of Jesus with someone today. The world is
dark and getting darker, but you are the light. Ask Holy Spirit
to reveal the power of His light to you. Today you will make the
difference in someone's life.

Day 18

God has made a way to escape

> There hath no temptation taken you but such
> as is common to man: but God is faithful, who
> will not suffer you to be tempted above that ye
> are able; but will with the temptation also make
> a way to escape, that ye may be able to bear it. (1
> Corinthians 10:13)

You will be tempted. Ask the Holy Spirit to show you the exit
door. God is faithful and knows how difficult temptation is. He
will bring you out.

Day 19

Receive God's grace

> And God is able to make all grace abound toward you; that ye, always having all sufficiency in all things, may abound to every good work. (2 Corinthians 9:8)

Thank God for His abundant grace. With His grace, you have everything you need to accomplish your assignment.

Day 20

Know that Jesus is your Healer

> Now when the sun was setting, all they that had
> any sick with divers diseases brought them unto
> him; and he laid his hands on every one of them,
> and healed them. (Luke 4:40)

Believe Jesus is your Healer. Plead the blood of Jesus over your
mind and body. Make the decree that there is nothing too hard
for Jesus. Expect miracles, and praise God, despite what you
feel or think.

Day 21

Use your tongue as a powerful weapon

> Death and life *are* in the power of the tongue:
> and they that love it shall eat the fruit thereof.
> (Proverbs 18:21)

Christian soldiers must speak life over their mind and body. Say what God has said about you. Speak and believe His Word over your life every day. Make it a habit, and you will see exponential growth in your spiritual life.

Day 22

Walk in the Spirit

> This I say then, Walk in the Spirit, and ye shall
> not fulfil the lust of the flesh. (Galatians 5:16)

Allow the Holy Spirit to teach you how to live an effective life. Depend on His guidance as He assists you through the daily challenges. Listen intently to His prompting. His leadership will help you navigate around the land mines of confusion, deception, and evil works.

Day 23

Praise God with all your heart

> By thee have I been holden up from the womb:
> thou art he that took me out of my mother's
> bowels: my praise *shall be* continually of thee.
> (Psalm 71:6)

Praise God with all your heart. God held you up in your mother's womb and brought you into the earth. Praise God for His goodness every day. Even in the hard times, reflect on God's love and mercy. Think about your testimony and all the things God has brought you through. Your praise will ambush the enemy.

Day 24

Soar today

> But they that wait upon the LORD shall renew
> *their* strength; they shall mount up with wings
> as eagles; they shall run, and not be weary; *and*
> they shall walk, and not faint. (Isaiah 40:31)

When eagles soar, they rely on rising air currents to gain altitude. You must rely upon the current of God to take you to the next level. Do not accept complacency or make excuses about your situation. Ask God to help you to depend on Him and to take you higher.

Day 25

Communicate properly

> But speaking the truth in love, may grow up into
> him in all things, which is the head, even Christ.
> (Ephesians 4:15)

Assess your attitude today. Learn how to talk to people in love, even when you don't agree with them. This isn't an easy task, but speaking the truth in love will honor God and help you maintain healthy relationships.

Day 26

Be a friend

> He that covereth a transgression seeketh love;
> but he that repeateth a matter separateth very
> friends. (Proverbs 17:9)

Are you trustworthy? This world needs people who are trustworthy. Be the person others can trust. Ask God to forgive you for the times you betrayed others. Receive His forgiveness, and ask Him to help you be a better friend.

Day 27

Use your time wisely

> Redeeming the time because the days are evil.
> (Ephesians 5:16)

Time is a gift from God so use it wisely. Take control of your day by acknowledging God and asking Him to direct your steps.

Day 28

Trust God for provision

> But my God shall supply all your need according
> to his riches in glory by Christ Jesus. (Philippians
> 4:19)

God will always make a way for you. Trust Him to provide
everything you need on your journey. There is no lack in Christ
Jesus. He will supply.

Day 29

Put your affections in the right place

> Set your affection on things above, not on things
> on the earth. (Colossians 3:2)

Earthly things will pass away because they are temporal. God is eternal. Make a conscious effort to set your affections on God. He will never fail you.

JUDITH GAFFNEY

Day 30

There is power in the blood of Jesus

> In him we have redemption through his blood,
> the forgiveness of sins, in accordance with the
> riches of God's grace. (Ephesians 1:7)

Take communion today, and thank Jesus for the blood He shed to liberate your soul. Walk in the power of the blood of Jesus. Plead the blood of Jesus over your life, and decree that you are redeemed and free. His blood cleanses us from every sin.

SUMMARY AND REFLECTION

Use this page to reflect and summarize
your boot camp experience.

Thank you for taking time to read and experience *Army Rise Up!*

May the blessing of our Lord Jesus Christ overtake you and cause you to triumph in every way.

Don't Give Up!

God is unstoppable. He is unbeatable, and He is truth. He will cross an ocean to save you and cause waters to spring up in a desert just for you. God's love for you is unconditional and abides forever. You are His delight.

The year 2020 started off very exciting for me. As an adjunct professor at Fashion Institute of Technology in New York, and the founder/fashion designer for Culture Trees, I had the opportunity to participate in FIT's 2020 Black History Month Exhibition Gallery/Fashion Show. When I spoke with the young woman who was planning the event, she was very excited about my brand, and informed me that I should bring my exhibit garments in the next day. I felt honored to have my garments in the FIT gallery and to be a participant in the fashion show.

The next morning, however, when I brought my garments to the gallery, one of the event coordinators said that I couldn't participate in the exhibition because all the mannequins were taken. The young woman I spoke to the day before was there and apologized. She said she didn't realize that there weren't enough mannequins. I was also informed that the available slots for the fashion show were filled. My heart dropped, and I did everything to fight the tears from falling down my face. I told the event coordinator that I was promised a space in the gallery, and I asked if there was anything I could do to participate. She said I had to get my own mannequin and then they would try to find a space for me. She also informed me that the mannequin had to be black.

I immediately told her that I would get a mannequin. I didn't even ask why I couldn't be in the fashion show. After that conversation, I left the college and hit the streets in Midtown Manhattan to search for a black mannequin. It was early February and very cold. I stopped by a familiar store that I thought might have mannequins, but they were out of business. While walking in the cold, I used my phone to search and call places that sold mannequins. The prices were exceptionally high and the delivery time was two or three days. I kept praying and asking Holy Spirit to show me where to go. I couldn't find a black mannequin anywhere.

I finally found a fabric store with a black mannequin in the window and asked the owner if I could borrow it for a Black History Month exhibition at FIT. After showing him my FIT identification card, he kindly allowed me to rent the mannequin for fifty dollars and keep it for four weeks. I quickly called an Uber and took the mannequin back to the college. When I arrived at FIT, the event coordinator was sitting in the lobby eating lunch with her friends. She looked at me with amazement and said, "You're back already?" I smiled, showed her the mannequin, and went inside the exhibition gallery to set it up. My garment was on exhibition in the FIT gallery for the next four weeks and seen by people from all over the world.

Never give up. Even when people make promises and change their mind, you must maintain an attitude of love and respect. Most importantly, have faith in God. He has given you a promise and purpose that enemy wants you to abandon. Press through, even if you must cry. Keep pressing, and continue to ask the Holy Spirit which way you should go. God will never fail you; He will cause doors that are closed to open just for you. God is strategic. Expect Him to move things for you.

Printed in the United States
by Baker & Taylor Publisher Services